AFC WEST

BY K. C. KELLEY

★ Denver Broncos ★ Kansas City Chiefs ★ Oakland Raiders ★ San Diego Chargers ★

Published by The Child's World®
1980 Lookout Drive
Mankato, MN 56003-1705
800-599-READ
www.childsworld.com

The Child's World®: Mary Berendes, Publishing Director
The Design Lab: Kathleen Petelinsek, Design
Editorial Directions, Inc.: Pam Mamsch and E. Russell Primm,
Project Managers

Photographs ©: Robbins Photography (except page 25, AP)

Library of Congress Cataloging-in-Publication Data
Kelley, K. C.
  AFC West / by K. C. Kelley.
    p. cm. Includes bibliographical references and index.
  ISBN 978-1-60973-130-4 (library reinforced : alk. paper)
  1. National Football League—History—Juvenile literature.
2. Football—United States—History—Juvenile literature. I. Title.
  GV955.5.N35K449 2011
  796.332'640973—dc22   2011007151

Printed in the United States of America
Mankato, MN
May, 2011
PA02093

TABLE OF
CONTENTS

AFC
WEST

4

First Season: 1960
NFL Championships: 2
Colors: Dark Blue and
Orange
Mascot: Miles

★

DENVER
BRONCOS

A MILE OF SMILES

Denver Broncos fans have put up with a lot. When the team started in 1960, they wore football's ugliest uniforms. Then Denver didn't have a winning record until 1973. And did we mention that the fans usually have to sit in cold winter weather to watch the games?

Once Denver started winning, they still fell short. The Broncos made it to four Super Bowls from 1977 through 1990—and lost all of them! But **loyal** Broncos fans stuck with them, filling Mile High Stadium with a sea of orange.

In the late 1990s, however, everything came together. Star quarterback John Elway had a terrific running back in Terrell Davis. The Broncos' defense was great. After many years of **big-game** losses, Denver won Super Bowl XXXII. Then they did it again the next year! Fans agreed it was worth the wait.

John Elway was the third quarterback in NFL history to pass for 45,000 yards.

HOME FIELD

The Broncos' home field gets its name from Denver's nickname. The city is located 1 mile (1.6 kilometers) above sea level. The Broncos play in Invesco Field at Mile High Stadium! Some visiting teams have trouble playing there. The air is thinner and can be harder to breathe that high up. Fans, however, have no trouble making lots of noise.

BIG DAYS

* Denver won its first American Football Conference (AFC) title in 1977. But the Broncos lost Super Bowl XII to Dallas.
* The Broncos won back-to-back Super Bowls, XXXII and XXXIII.
* John Elway was named the MVP in the second one, which was his final NFL game.
* Jake "The Snake" Plummer led Denver to the AFC title game in 2005.

Invesco Field can seat up to 76,125 Broncos fans on game days.

SUPERSTARS!

★

THEN

John Elway, quarterback: one of NFL's greatest passers and a fiery leader

Tom Jackson, linebacker: hard-nosed defender who has become a well-known TV guy

Floyd Little, running back: tough to tackle, a solid Denver running back for nine years

★

NOW

Champ Bailey, cornerback: one of the best in the NFL at covering receivers

Kyle Orton, quarterback: young and strong — can he be the next Elway?

D. J. Williams, linebacker: sack-happy defender follows great Denver tradition

★

STAT LEADERS

(All-time team leaders*)

Passing Yards: John Elway, 51,475
Rushing Yards: Terrell Davis, 7,607
Receiving Yards: Rod Smith, 11,389
Touchdowns: Rod Smith, 71
Interceptions: Steve Foley, 44

★

(*Through 2010 season.)

TIMELINE

1960
Broncos are one of the first teams in the new American Football League (AFL).

1970
AFL teams, including the Broncos, join the NFL.

1977
Broncos win their first AFC championship.

1986
Broncos make the first of three Super Bowls in four years; they lose all three of them.

Linebacker D.J. Williams has had four 100-tackle seasons.

1997

Denver wins first Super Bowl, defeating the Green Bay Packers 31–24.

1998

Denver sets a team record with 14 wins and captures its second Super Bowl in a row; John Elway retires after winning the game's MVP award.

2005

Denver makes it to the AFC Championship Game for the eighth time.

First Season: 1960
AFL/NFL
   Championships: 3
Colors: Red, Gold, and
   White
Mascot: KC Wolf

★

KANSAS CITY
CHIEFS

GREAT ONCE . . . GREAT AGAIN?

The Chiefs were one of the best teams in the AFL. The AFL started in 1960 to challenge the older NFL. (All of the teams in the AFC West started in the AFL.) The Chiefs weren't the Chiefs in 1960, however. They were the Dallas Texans. In 1962, they won the AFL title. The next year, they moved to Kansas City and took on their new name.

The Chiefs won the 1966 AFL title, too. Then they played in the very first Super Bowl, against the Green Bay Packers of the NFL. The Packers won, but the Chiefs liked the big game. They came back three seasons later and won Super Bowl IV!

The Chiefs and other AFL teams joined the NFL in 1970. The 1990s were a great decade for the Chiefs. The team has had tough years recently, but young stars have fans looking ahead with hope.

Quarterback Matt Cassel played four seasons with the New England Patriots before joining the Chiefs in 2009.

HOME FIELD

Arrowhead Stadium is always packed on game days. From 1991 through early 2010, the team sold out every seat for every game—155 in a row! The crowd wears the team's main color and looks like a sea of red cheering for the Chiefs.

BIG DAYS

★ A last-play **field goal** won the AFL title for the Dallas Texans in 1962.

★ In 1969, the Chiefs became the second AFL team to win the Super Bowl. They beat the Minnesota Vikings 23–7.

★ On their way to a team-record 13 wins in 1997, the Chiefs had the top-ranked offense in the NFL.

Arrowhead Stadium has been the Chiefs' home since 1972.

SUPERSTARS!

★

THEN

Bobby Bell, linebacker: hard-hitting tackler who
anchored the 1960s defense
Len Dawson, quarterback: Hall of Famer led the team
to the Super Bowl IV title
Christian Okoye, running back: powerful African-born
runner nicknamed "Nigerian Nightmare"

★

NOW

Dwayne Bowe, wide receiver: speedy with great leaping ability
Matt Cassel, quarterback: former baseball pitcher turned
strong-armed passer
Jamaal Charles, running back: latest in a long line of great runners

★

STAT LEADERS

(All-time team leaders*)
Passing Yards: Len Dawson, 28,507
Rushing Yards: Priest Holmes, 6,070
Receiving Yards: Tony Gonzalez, 10,940
Touchdowns: Mark Clayton, 82
Interceptions: Emmitt Thomas, 58

★

(*Through 2010 season.)

TIMELINE

1960
Team starts play as the Dallas Texans in
the new AFL.

1962
Texans win AFL championship over
Houston in a thrilling **overtime**
game.

1963
Team moves to Kansas City and becomes
the Chiefs.

Wide receiver Dwayne Bowe was a first-round draft pick for the Chiefs in 2007.

1966
Chiefs win AFL championship but lose Super Bowl I to Green Bay.

1970
Chiefs beat the Vikings to win Super Bowl IV.

1990–1997
Chiefs have at least 10 wins in six of eight seasons.

16

First Season: 1960
AFL/NFL
    Championships: 4
Colors: Silver and Black
Mascot: None

★

OAKLAND
RAIDERS

BEWARE THE PIRATES OF THE NFL!

Their fans wear skulls and wild costumes. Their logo is
a pirate. And their players are often among the
toughest in the NFL. The Oakland Raiders are one of
the best-known teams in the league. They're famous
for their **fierceness** but also for their excellent play. The
Raiders have played in five Super Bowls and won three.

One man has been the face of the Raiders for years.
In 1963, Al Davis took over as head coach. (The Raiders
were in the AFL then.) He only coached three seasons,
but he's been with the team ever since. Today, he's the
team owner. Davis helped create the teams that won
Super Bowls in 1977, 1981, and 1984.

The Raiders moved to Los Angeles in 1982 and played
there until 1994. While they were there, they won Super
Bowl XVIII. They moved back to Oakland in 1995. Their
loyal fans were happy to have the "silver and black"
back home!

Running back Darren McFadden was a runner-up for
the Heisman Trophy two times during his college career.

HOME FIELD

The Oakland Coliseum is the site of a costume party every Raiders game day. Many fans dress up in wild outfits of silver and black. It's Halloween every game day. The Coliseum is also home to the Oakland A's baseball team. Many of the Raiders games are played with the baseball infield dirt on parts of the football field.

BIG DAYS

★ The Raiders won the 1967 AFL title but lost Super Bowl II to Green Bay.
★ Oakland won Super Bowl XI, defeating the Minnesota Vikings.
★ The Raiders brought a Super Bowl title to their second home, Los Angeles. They beat the Washington Redskins to win Super Bowl XVIII.

The Raiders played their first game in Oakland Coliseum against the Kansas City Chiefs on September 18, 1966.

SUPERSTARS!

★

THEN

Marcus Allen, running back: superfast, hard to bring down,
and a great runner

Ted Hendricks, linebacker: "the Stork" was huge and hard to get around

Daryle Lamonica, quarterback: great passer known as the Mad
Bomber for his long passes

★

NOW

Jason Campbell, quarterback: a strong arm that reaches
the team's speedy receivers

Darren McFadden, running back: a great runner but also
a great pass catcher

Zach Miller, tight end: a **dependable** receiver and powerful blocker

★

STAT LEADERS

(All-time team leaders*)

Passing Yards: Ken Stabler, 19,078

Rushing Yards: Marcus Allen, 8,545

Receiving Yards: Tim Brown, 14,734

Touchdowns: Tim Brown, 104

Interceptions: Lester Hayes and Willie Brown, 39

★

(*Through 2010 season.)

TIMELINE

1960	1967	1968	1976	1982
Oakland Raiders start play as a member of the new AFL.	Team wins the AFL title but loses Super Bowl II.	Raiders lose AFL Championship Game; they are runners-up in six of eight seasons (1968–1975).	Oakland wins Super Bowl XI over the Vikings.	Team moves to Los Angeles and plays in the Coliseum.

Quarterback Jason Campbell has six career 300-yard passing games.

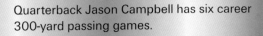

1983	**1995**	**2000**	**2002**	**2003**
Raiders win Super Bowl XVIII, beating the Redskins.	Raiders move back to Oakland.	They lose the AFC Championship Game to the Baltimore Ravens.	Team loses Super Bowl XXXVII to the Tampa Bay Buccaneers.	Raiders begin an NFL-record streak of losing 11 or more games in a season.

First Season: 1960
NFL Championships: 0
Colors: Blue and Gold
Mascot: Boltman

★

SAN DIEGO
CHARGERS

THE SAN DIEGO AIR SHOW

The Chargers were part of the AFL from the beginning. More than any other team, they loved to pass. Their **high-flying** style was popular with fans. The team won the 1963 AFL title. Other teams soon started passing more. The Chargers' style of play helped change the NFL.

The Chargers kept passing after they joined the NFL in 1970. Quarterback Dan Fouts was one of the first to reach 4,000 passing yards in a season. Many receivers piled up catch after catch for San Diego. The Chargers were very good but always fell short of the title.

In the 1980s, the team lost two AFC Championship Games. In 1994, they reached Super Bowl XXIX but lost to San Francisco. San Diego lost the 2007 AFC title game, too. Today's Chargers are still a top team, looking to win the ultimate game.

Running back LaDainian Tomlinson has averaged over four yards per carry in his ten-year NFL career.

HOME FIELD

Chargers fans live in one of the most beautiful cities in the world. The team's games can sometimes seem like a giant beach party, with football thrown in for fun. The excellent weather in San Diego makes Qualcomm Stadium a great place to hang out on fall Sundays. Look for fans working on their tans between plays.

BIG DAYS

★ The Chargers won the 1963 AFL Championship. Their passing skills helped them pound the Buffalo Patriots 51–10.

★ San Diego earned its first AFC title in 1994. The team lost Super Bowl XXIX to the San Francisco 49ers 49–26.

★ After winning the AFC West, the Chargers reached the 2007 AFC Championship Game. They lost to the Patriots 21–12.

More than 70,000 Chargers fans can enjoy home games at Qualcomm Stadium.

SUPERSTARS!

★

THEN

Dan Fouts, quarterback: one of the NFL's strongest passers
Junior Seau, linebacker: powerful tackler who led the team's defense for 13 seasons
LaDainian "LT" Tomlinson, running back: set NFL touchdown record in 2006 with 31 TDs

★

NOW

Antonio Gates, tight end: future Hall of Famer who set a single-season TD record for tight ends (13 in 2004)
Ryan Mathews, running back: young star trying to take over for LT
Philip Rivers, quarterback: continues a great tradition of strong San Diego passers

★

STAT LEADERS

(All-time team leaders*)
Passing Yards: Dan Fouts, 43,040
Rushing Yards: LaDainian Tomlinson, 12,490
Receiving Yards: Lance Alworth, 9,584
Touchdowns: LaDainian Tomlinson, 153
Interceptions: Gill Byrd, 42

★

(*Through 2010 season.)

TIMELINE

1960
Chargers are one of the teams in the new AFL.

1963
Chargers win the AFL championship, beating Boston 51-10.

1980
Chargers lose the first of two straight AFC Championship Games.

Quarterback Philip Rivers led the NFL in 2010 with 4,710 passing yards.

1994

Defeating the Steelers, the Chargers win the AFC championship but then lose Super Bowl XXIX.

2007

San Diego wins the AFC West but loses the AFC Championship Game.

STAT
STUFF

★

AFC WEST DIVISION STATISTICS*

Team	All-Time Record (W-L-T)	NFL Titles (Most Recent)	Times in NFL Playoffs
Denver Broncos	415–379–10	2 (1998)	17
Kansas City Chiefs	403–379–12	3 (1969)	16
Oakland Raiders	443–361–11	4 (1983)	21
San Diego Chargers	394–393–11	1 (1963)	17

★

AFC WEST DIVISION CHAMPIONSHIPS (MOST RECENT)

Denver Broncos . . . 11 (2005)
Kansas City Chiefs . . . 6 (2010)
Oakland Raiders . . . 12 (2002)
San Diego Chargers . . . 9 (2007)

★

(*Through 2010 season; includes AFL statistics.)

Position Key:
QB: Quarterback
RB: Running back
WR: Wide receiver
TE: Tight end
C: Center
T: Tackle
G: Guard
CB: Cornerback
LB: Linebacker
DE: Defensive end
K: Kicker

28

AFC WEST PRO FOOTBALL
HALL OF FAME MEMBERS

Denver Broncos
Willie Brown, CB
John Elway, QB
Floyd Little, RB
Shannon Sharpe, TE
Gary Zimmerman, T

Kansas City Chiefs
Marcus Allen, RB
Bobby Bell, LB
Junious (Buck) Buchanan, DE
Len Dawson, QB
Lamar Hunt, Owner
Willie Lanier, LB
Marv Levy, Coach
Jan Stenerud, K
Hank Stram, Coach
Derrick Thomas, LB
Emmitt Thomas, CB

Oakland Raiders
Marcus Allen, RB
Fred Biletnikoff, WR
George Blanda, QB, K

Bob (Boomer) Brown, T
Willie Brown, CB
Dave Casper, TE
Al Davis, Coach, Owner
Mike Haynes, CB
Ted Hendricks, LB
Howie Long, DE
John Madden, Coach
Jim Otto, C
Jerry Rice, WR
Art Shell, T
Gene Upshaw, G

San Diego Chargers
Lance Alworth, WR
Fred Dean, DE
Dan Fouts, QB
Sid Gillman, Coach
Charlie Joiner, WR
Ron Mix, T
Kellen Winslow, TE

NOTE: Includes players with at least three seasons with the team. Players may appear with more than one team.

GLOSSARY

⭐

big game (BIG GAME): common nickname for the Super Bowl

dependable (di-PEND-uh-bl): able to be relied upon

field goal (FEELD GOHL): a kick that starts from the field and goes between the uprights; worth three points

fierceness (FIHRSS-nuhss): performing with power and force

high-flying (HYE FLY-engh): very successful or determined to succeed

loyal (LOI-uhl): faithful, supportive

overtime (OH-vur-time): extra time added to a game when the score is tied at the end of the normal playing time

FIND OUT MORE

★

BOOKS

Buckley, James Jr. *Scholastic Ultimate Guide to Football*. New York: Franklin Watts, 2009.

Jacobs, Greg. *The Everything Kids' Football Book*. Avon, MA: Adams Media, 2010.

Stewart, Mark. *The Denver Broncos*. Chicago: Norwood House Press, 2007.

Stewart, Mark. *The Kansas City Chiefs*. Chicago: Norwood House Press, 2009.

Stewart, Mark. *The Oakland Raiders*. Chicago: Norwood House Press, 2010.

Stewart, Mark, and Jason Aikens. *The San Diego Chargers*. Chicago: Norwood House Press, 2009.

★

WEB SITES

For links to learn more about football visit

www.childsworld.com/links

Note to Parents, Teachers, and Librarians: We routinely verify our Web links to make sure they are safe and active sites. So encourage your readers to check them out!

INDEX

ABOUT THE AUTHOR

K.C. Kelley has written dozens of books about sports for young readers, including several on football. He used to work for the NFL and has covered several Super Bowls. He helped start NFL.com and still watches games every Sunday, all season long!